MW01165089

SAINT ANTHONY OF PADUA

Catholic Story Coloring Book

This is his story, written by Mary Fabyan Windeatt
With pictures for you to color, drawn by Gedge Harmon

This book belongs to

_____

*The pictures in this book can be colored
with crayons, markers or water colors.*

TAN BOOKS AND PUBLISHERS, INC., ROCKFORD, ILLINOIS 61105

CHAPTER ONE

DON Martin De Bulhom, chief magistrate of the Portuguese city of Lisbon, leapt briskly from his horse. He was in excellent spirits on this bright spring morning in the year 1207, for his men had just captured a band of pagan Saracens who had been terrorizing the whole countryside.

"Teresa!" he called exultantly. "Ferdinand!"

Wide-eyed with joy, Don Martin's wife and twelve-year-old son came hurrying into the courtyard. "Oh, Martin! Thank God you're safe!"

"How many prisoners this time, Father?"

Don Martin chuckled. "Better than usual, son. Six hundred."

That same night the De Bulhom castle was gay with lights and music as Don Martin presided at a great victory banquet. But young Ferdinand sat strangely silent amid the festive proceedings. Since 792, he reflected, cruel Mohammedans from North Africa had been trying to stamp out the Christian faith in Portugal. Saracens they were called, and if they should ever succeed in their efforts. . . .

"Well, boy, why so serious?" demanded Don Martin jovially.

Ferdinand hesitated. "I . . . I was just wondering, sir."

"Wondering what, lad? Speak up!"

"If . . . if next time you'd let me go to fight the Saracens, too. Oh, Father, I'd like so much to help!"

SAINT ANTHONY OF PADUA

LOUD cheers greeted the boy's words, although Dona Teresa could take no pleasure in them now or later. What a pity that men must fight and kill, she thought, even though it be for a worthy cause! Surely if all the mothers of the world could have their way—

"Now, now, you mustn't worry about the future," said Father Peter one day. "Something tells me that Ferdinand will never be a soldier."

Dona Teresa stared. This priest from the Augustinian monastery in Lisbon was a holy man, of course. And one who had taught her boy for several years. But surely he didn't mean—

"Yes, I do mean it," said Father Peter, reading her thoughts. "Now that Ferdinand's fifteen, I'm almost certain God is calling him to the religious life. For instance, just look out there in the garden."

Dona Teresa turned, then gasped. Ferdinand had always been a good lad, but now the fervent way in which he was praying before Our Lady's shrine—

"I . . . I don't understand!" she exclaimed, her eyes shining. "If he really wants to be a priest, why hasn't he told his father? Or me?"

Father Peter shrugged. "Perhaps he's afraid, Dona Teresa. After all, hasn't Don Martin always expected him to take over his own work some day?"

CHAPTER THREE

DON MARTIN could not conceal his disappointment when Ferdinand made known his desire to enter God's service. However, he did not withhold his consent.

"Maybe you're right, son," he muttered. "Maybe you can do more for Portugal as a priest than as a soldier. But I find that rather hard to believe, with the Saracens ready to murder us in our very beds."

The fifteen-year-old boy tried not to be hurt by his father's bluntness. How dreadful to be thought a coward! Worse still, to feel that he himself was responsible for his father's attitude, since from childhood he had led him to believe that he really wanted to be a soldier. But in the last three years, ever since God's call had come—

"I ... I'm sorry, Father," he choked. "Please believe me!"

God blessed Ferdinand's decision to study for the priesthood, and soon he had settled down happily in the monastery of the Canons Regular of Saint Augustine in Lisbon. Indeed, on July 16, 1212, when the Saracens suffered a crushing defeat at Las Navas, he experienced a sense of real triumph. Surely his prayers and sacrifices had helped to merit the victory? Then eight years later, in Coimbra, he knew even greater joy. Once again Don Martin had come to visit him, to apologize for his former harshness, to kneel for the blessing of the King of Kings!

SAINT ANTHONY OF PADUA

CHAPTER FOUR

NOW that he was a priest of God, twenty-five-year-old Ferdinand prayed more fervently than ever that the cruel Saracens would never again enter Portugal to murder and destroy.

"If only there were missionaries to go to them in North Africa, to help them to know and love the True Faith!" he mused.

But few in Coimbra believed that the enemy could be converted. After all, didn't Father Ferdinand remember that several months before, on January 16, 1220, five missionaries had been cruelly murdered by the Saracens in North Africa? They had been members of the Friars Minor (a religious group recently founded in Italy by a certain Francis of Assisi), and rumor had it that even now their remains were on the way to Coimbra.

Ferdinand nodded calmly. "Yes, I've heard about those good men. And I'm quite sure of one thing."

"What, Father?"

"Despite the great risk, other men ought to take their place."

This conviction grew stronger with the passing weeks. But when the casket containing all that remained of the martyred friars finally arrived in Coimbra, Ferdinand could only kneel before it in speechless wonder.

"You, too, are going to go to Africa!" a mysterious voice was saying in his heart. "You, too, are going to be a Friar Minor!"

SAINT ANTHONY OF PADUA

FOR a moment the young priest stirred uneasily. Was he dreaming? Or was he merely the victim of his own imagination? Then, as the mysterious voice continued to speak, he realized the truth. He was not to spend his days in the prayerful seclusion of an Augustinian monastery. Instead, he was to be a missionary in the new religious Order founded by Francis of Assisi. And his first field of labor was to be among the Saracens in North Africa.

"Nonsense!" exclaimed his Augustinian superiors when he had made his decision known to them. "Why, those heathen wouldn't give you a chance to work for them, Father! They'd kill you the first day."

Ferdinand smiled. "What of that? Then I'd be a martyr."

"But . . . but this is fantastic!"

"Possibly. Just the same, may I have a dispensation to leave this house and join the Friars Minor? I'm sure that's what God wants."

With considerable reluctance the Augustinians arranged for the dispensation, and on the day appointed Ferdinand set out for Olivares, on the outskirts of Coimbra, where two Friars Minor were waiting for him in the little chapel that was their headquarters.

"How good God is to let me be a missionary!" thought Ferdinand as he knelt to receive the habit of his new religious family. "How very good!"

SAINT ANTHONY OF PADUA

BUT it was not just a new habit, or the love and friendship of new spiritual brothers, which Ferdinand received at Olivares. He also received a new name, that of Anthony, the holy Egyptian hermit of the fourth century who was the patron saint of the little chapel.

"Well, Father, how do you feel now?" asked one of the friars jokingly. "Do you still want to go to Africa?"

Anthony's eyes shone. "Oh, yes!" he burst out. "The sooner the better!"

But a few weeks later, when he was finally permitted to set out as a missionary, Anthony felt less confident. The life of a Friar Minor was far harder than he had thought. True, there was a marvelous sense of freedom in having no material security, in being utterly dependent on Providence for food and drink and shelter, but would the severity of the Holy Rule leave him strength to preach to the Saracens, even to reach their country?

The answer came in the spring of 1221, shortly after Anthony had landed at the North African port of Ceuta. Then, burning with fever and utterly exhausted, he collapsed in the street before he had preached a single sermon!

"Father, you're coming back with me to Portugal," said a passing sea captain grimly. "Don't you know you're a very sick man?"

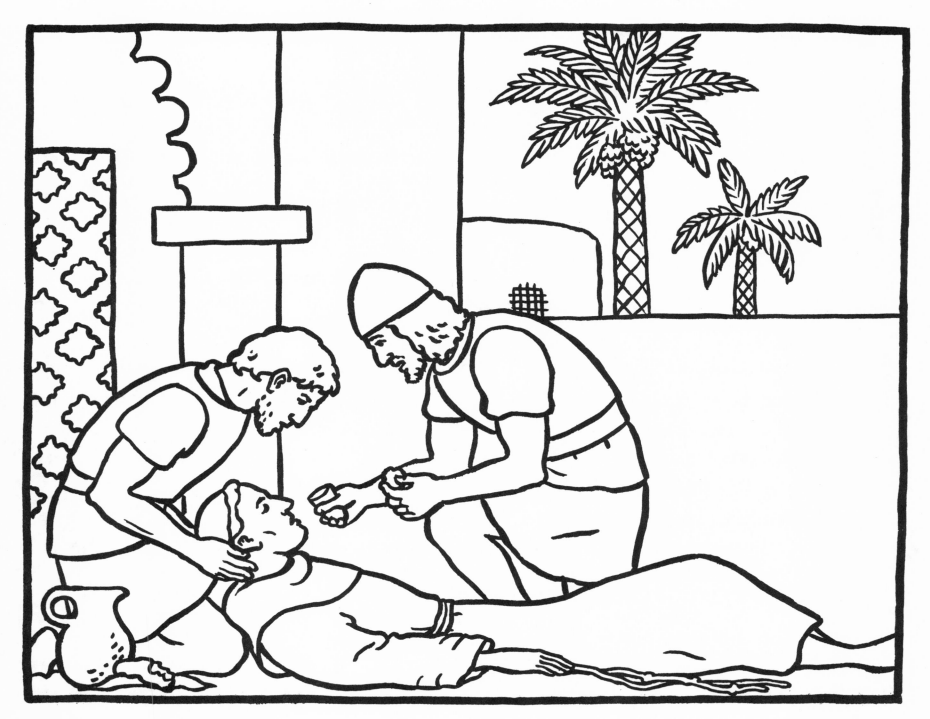

SAINT ANTHONY OF PADUA

CHAPTER SEVEN

ANTHONY groaned. Return to Portugal now? "No, no!" he whispered feebly. "It's God's Will that I give my life for the Saracens. . . ."

But the captain paid no heed. Aided by a member of the crew, he helped Anthony to take some nourishment, then carried him down to the waterfront. "We're sailing for home in a little while," he said kindly. "Just relax now, Father. Everything's going to be all right."

Bitter disappointment filled the young priest's heart. What a fool he had been to think he was worthy of missionary work! To have dreamed of winning heaven through martyrdom!

"Dear God, forgive my pride!" he murmured, then drifted into a deep sleep.

Some hours later he awoke to find that the ship was on the high seas. But even as he considered what the future might hold for him now—a stupid friar who had failed on his first assignment—the ship gave a violent shudder, then lurched perilously to one side.

"Don't worry, Father," called one of the crew cheerfully. "It's just a bit of bad weather." But by nightfall the captain reported that a dangerous hurricane had come up, and that the ship was no longer heading northwest to Portugal through the Strait of Gibraltar but eastward into the Mediterranean.

"You'd better start praying, Father," he growled. "We're in a bad way."

SAINT ANTHONY OF PADUA

CHAPTER EIGHT

THE captain spoke the truth. For several days, far off her course, the ship tossed about like a matchstick in the giant waves. Everyone felt that only a miracle could save them, and ceaselessly Anthony stormed heaven for help. Then one afternoon, after more than a week had passed, the wind died away and the captain pointed a shaking finger to the right. "Land!" he gasped eagerly. "The island of Sicily, Father! We . . . we're saved!"

The next morning, weak and shaken though he was, Anthony managed to offer Mass at the chapel of the Friars Minor in Messina, the island's capital. What the future had in store for him he still did not know, but surely there was no point now in returning to Portugal with the captain and his crew? Surely God had sent him to Sicily so that he might work for souls there? However, after he had rested a bit, his fellow-religious explained that their Father Guardian was attending a General Chapter of the Order at Assisi, and that no assignment could be issued without his permission.

"If you feel strong enough, Father, why don't you go to Assisi, too?" they urged. "Just think, you might meet Friar Francis himself!"

Anthony's heart beat fast. What an unlooked-for privilege! "I'll leave right away," he decided. "Thank you, my brothers—thank you for everything!"

SAINT ANTHONY OF PADUA

CHAPTER NINE

BUT the four-hundred-mile trip, even though he was accompanied by one of the friars from Messina, was almost too much for Anthony's weakened body. Day by day he was forced to slow his pace, so that he did not arrive at the General Chapter until the last session was in progress. Then, having caught but a mere glimpse of Friar Francis, he found that all the assignments had been given out and that everyone would soon be leaving.

"What shall I do now?" he wondered uneasily. "Where shall I go?"

Suddenly a certain Father Gratian approached. "Is anything wrong?" he asked kindly. "You don't look at all well."

Since his questioner was the Provincial of the Roman Province, Anthony did not hesitate to tell his whole miserable story: how he had hoped to work among the Saracens in North Africa, how his health had broken and he was forced to set out again for Portugal. He described the terrible storm at sea, the almost miraculous arrival at Messina. . . .

Father Gratian listened in amazement, then clapped Anthony on the back. "I have just the place for you," he said briskly. "It's a little retreat near Arezzo dedicated to Saint Paul. There are three men there now, but it seems they need a fourth—someone to do the cooking."

Anthony's heart skipped a beat. He, a cook? But almost before he knew it, he was happily settled down at his new work.

SAINT ANTHONY OF PADUA

CHAPTER TEN

A YEAR passed, and Anthony knew that he had never experienced such peace and joy. True, his little community was extremely poor in this world's goods, but what of that? The Christian love and understanding at the small house near Arezzo were beyond description in words. As for the solitude—ah, what a blessing when it came time to pray!

Then one day Father Gratian sent word that Anthony and his fellow-religious were to go to Forli (some forty miles to the southeast), to assist at the Ordination of certain Friars Minor. Obediently the group set out, being joined on the way by some Friars Preachers, the spiritual sons of Father Dominic de Guzman, of whom several were also to be ordained.

Anthony's eyes shone. What a privilege to hear a sermon by one of these brothers in Christ after the Ordination service! Although their Order was still very young, the Friars Preachers were famous throughout Italy and France for their ability to explain the Word of God. Strangely enough, however, when it came time for the sermon, no black-and-white-clad Friar Preacher appeared in the pulpit.

"Father, there's been a terrible mix-up!" Anthony's superior whispered nervously. "No one here seems prepared to speak. Quick, couldn't you say a few words?"

SAINT ANTHONY OF PADUA

CHAPTER ELEVEN

ANTHONY drew back in dismay. A man who spent his days among the pots and pans should address the congregation on this important occasion? Unprepared, and before the Bishop? What a horror! Yet remembering his vow of obedience—

"V-very well," he stammered. "I . . . I'll try."

With a fervent prayer for enlightenment, he rose to his feet. At first the words came slowly, but as he warmed to his subject—the holy priesthood—his hearers looked at one another in astonishment. What splendid delivery! What marvelous understanding of the priestly calling!

"You'd better go to Vercelli for higher studies," declared Father Gratian when he heard about what had happened. "Why, I had no idea you had such a way with words!"

Soon Anthony was making hundreds of friends by the power of his sermons. And in 1224, when obedience sent him to preach in France, he made hundreds more. But presently a jealous youth decided that Anthony's success as a preacher was in some way related to his daily reading from a certain book.

"If I could learn what's in that book, I could be famous, too," he told himself. And so, when no one was looking, he slipped into Anthony's cell and made off with his well-worn breviary.

SAINT ANTHONY OF PADUA

CHAPTER TWELVE

ANTHONY was frantic when he discovered his loss. All books were precious, of course, but a priest's breviary—with the various prayers he must say each day . . . the many useful notes which he himself had made in the margins of his own copy. . . .

"Oh, this is terrible!" he moaned. "Dear Lord, what'll I do?"

Even as Anthony stormed heaven for help, the thief was happily nearing home. A brief glance at the prize tucked under his arm had already revealed the many explanatory notes written on almost every page. Ah, to make this valuable information his own and win a following that would bring him both fame and fortune! But as he prepared to cross a certain bridge, a terrible monster suddenly blocked the way. Growling and snorting, its clawlike hands wielding a huge axe, it crouched to spring.

"No, no!" screamed the terrified youth. "Dear God, don't l-let it t-touch me! Oh, Father Anthony, I'll b-bring back your b-book!" And turning, he ran, and never stopped running until he had reached the house of the Friars Minor.

"P-please forgive me, Father!" he burst out, throwing himself at Anthony's feet. "I w-won't ever s-steal from anyone again!"

SAINT ANTHONY OF PADUA

CHAPTER THIRTEEN

HAD the monster been the Devil? No one could be sure. Because of what had happened, however, Anthony's prayers were soon in great demand for the return of lost or stolen articles.

"The good friar is a saint," one person told another earnestly. "God blesses every request he makes."

Anthony merely laughed when such reports reached his ears. "Everyone is a saint who really tries to do God's Will," he said cheerfully. "And if he keeps on trying, he may even be a great saint."

Presently the French city of Bourges became the scene of Anthony's labors. For many years heresy had been at work here, so that thousands of people no longer accepted certain important truths of the Christian faith. Thus, one day while Anthony was preaching in the marketplace—

"Don't try to tell me that God Himself is present in the Blessed Sacrament!" exclaimed a certain merchant scornfully. "Why, the Host is just ordinary bread!"

Anthony shuddered. "Sir, your mule doesn't agree."

"W-what?"

"You heard me. Bring the beast here three days from now, and you'll see what I mean."

SAINT ANTHONY OF PADUA

CHAPTER FOURTEEN

THE man paled. How had Anthony guessed the irreligious scheme he had in mind? "V-very well," he muttered nervously. "It's a bargain."

Soon the whole story was out. Three days from now Anthony would bring the Blessed Sacrament into the marketplace and command the mule to adore its Maker. Only if it obeyed would the merchant believe in the Real Presence. However, food must be offered to the mule while Anthony was speaking. And since the poor beast would have eaten nothing in the meantime—

"What a test!" laughed the heretics of Bourges. "And to think the friar was fool enough to agree to it!"

The city's few believers were more than anxious as they gathered in the marketplace on the morning of the day appointed. Surely Father Anthony had gone too far in practically demanding a miracle from heaven? Then suddenly their fears were forgotten. The friar had just come from Mass, a sacred Host in his hand, to confront the merchant and his mule. . . .

"Poor beast of burden, adore your Lord and your God!"

"Here, stupid, eat your oats!"

For an instant the hungry animal looked from one man to the other. Then slowly, with bowed head, it knelt at Anthony's feet.

SAINT ANTHONY OF PADUA

CHAPTER FIFTEEN

BY nightfall word of the wonder had spread throughout the city. Thousands of heretics flocked to Anthony to profess a belief in all the teachings of the Church (even as the merchant had now done), and to ask his prayers. In fact, by the fall of 1226, the thirty-one-year-old Portuguese friar had become one of Europe's most famous missionaries.

Presently Anthony was ordered to preach in the Italian city of Padua, where he was deeply grateful for God's continued blessing on his work. How many friends he had here! What crowds came to his sermons! Yet, one hundred and twenty-five miles to the southeast, in the seaport town of Rimini, heresy was as strong as it had ever been in France. . . .

"I must go to Rimini," he decided one day. "Even if I make only one convert there, the trip will have been worthwhile."

But very quickly Anthony discovered that the people of Rimini were not of a mind to listen to sermons. Greatly discouraged, he set out for an isolated cliff overlooking the harbor. What should he do now? Where should he go? Then suddenly he gasped. Thousands of fish were swarming up through the waters of the Adriatic to range themselves before him in ordered rows!

For a moment he stared in silence. Then, eyes shining, he flung wide his arms. "You, little brothers, will hear what I have to say!" he cried joyfully. "You will listen to the Word of God which men refuse to heed. . . ."

SAINT ANTHONY OF PADUA

CHAPTER SIXTEEN

IN a matter of minutes Anthony was pouring out his heart. What a thought that God should love the souls He had created far more than they could love themselves! That He was willing to forgive all their sins, no matter how serious! In fact, he soon became so carried away by the immensity of God's goodness that he failed to notice the approach of certain farmers on their way to market. Thus, when he had finished his sermon—

"Oh, Father, we heard every word!"

"A miracle! God be praised!"

"Yes, yes! You'll have no more trouble in Rimini, Father!"

It was true. Convinced that a saint had come among them, the people of Rimini now willingly listened to all of Anthony's sermons, so that before long the entire city had been converted.

"Preach to us, too!" begged all his friends in Padua, when he returned to his headquarters there. "Please, Father!"

So Anthony preached in and about the beloved city of his adoption until the year 1231, when his health began to fail. And as he knelt grieving one night over his inability to work any longer for souls, the Child Jesus appeared. "Soon you will be with Me in paradise," He said comfortingly.

The heart of the thirty-six-year-old friar leapt for joy. How glorious the Child was! And what a grace to have been His missionary!